Herbs and Medicinal Plants in Cross–Stitch

GERDA BENGTSSON

Herbs and Medicinal Plants in Cross–Stitch

from the Danish Handcraft Guild

VAN NOSTRAND REINHOLD COMPANY
NEW YORK   CINCINNATI   TORONTO   LONDON   MELBOURNE

Copyright © 1978 by
Selskabet til Haandarbejdets Fremme and
Høst & Søns Forlag, Copenhagen.
Library of Congress Catalog Card Number 78-8618
ISBN 0-442-20677-1

Printed in Denmark

Published in 1979
by Van Nostrand Reinhold Company
A division of Litton Educational Publishing, Inc.
135 West 50th Street, New York, NY 10020, U.S.A.

Van Nostrand Reinhold Limited
1410 Birchmount Road
Scarborough, Ontario M1P 2E7, Canada

Van Nostrand Reinhold Australia Pty. Ltd.
17 Queen Street
Mitcham, Victoria 3132, Australia

Van Nostrand Reinhold Company Limited
Molly Millars Lane
Wokingham, Berkshire, England

16 15 14 13 12 11 10 9 8 7 6 5 4 3 2 1

Library of Congress Cataloging in Publication Data
Bengtsson, Gerda.
Herbs and medicinal plants in cross-stitch from
the Danish Handcraft Guild.

1. Cross-stitch-Patterns. 2. Design, Decora-
tive-Plant forms. 3. Herbs. 4. Materia medica,
Vegetable. I. Danish Handcraft Guild. II. Title.
TT778.C76B46133   746.4'4   78-8618
ISBN 0-442-20677-1

Contents

Preface

The flowers from Gerda Bengtsson's 1975 and 1977 calendars, now sold out, have been collected together in this little book. The continued interest in these motifs has been so great that the Danish Handcraft Guild has decided to reissue them.

Quite apart from Gerda Bengtsson's extremely decorative interpretation of the various herbs, the motifs appear to me to contain an element of surprise – the surprise that lies in the discovery that, behind the names usually associated with the dried powders or corns in small bags and jars to be found in the kitchen or medicine cabinets, there are some beautiful, flowering plants.

Gertie Wandel

Materials and instructions

The motifs in this book will look their best if sewn on linen with 30 threads to the inch, referred to in this book as linen 12, or on a slightly coarser quality with 27 threads to the inch (linen 10). With the exception of the Foxglove (see page 37), they will appear too coarse if worked on linen with 18 threads to the inch (linen 7). The linen must of course have the same number of threads in both directions.

The chart on page 7 summarizes all the necessary information.

The types of linen used, with the corresponding thread and needles are:

Linen 12, bleached: 30 threads to the inch, 64 inches wide (160 cm). It is worked with 1 strand of Danish Flower Thread using tapestry needle no. 24.

Linen 10, bleached: 27 threads to the inch, 60 inches wide (150 cm). It is worked with 1 strand of Danish Flower Thread using tapestry needle no. 22.

Linen 7, bleached: 18 threads to the inch, 56 inches wide (140 cm). It is worked with 2 strands of Danish Flower Thread using tapestry needle no. 20.

On all the patterns the center lines are indicated by arrows. The actual center of the pattern lies at the intersection of these two lines.
One square on the pattern is equivalent to two threads on the linen. The motifs are worked with Danish Handcraft Guild's Flower Thread, which is a fine, mat, cotton yarn in beautiful, natural shades.
In a few cases shiny, white DMC Thread is used. Linen 12 and linen 10 are worked with two strands of DMC Thread and linen 7 with four strands. See the color chart on page 9.

From the chart below, it is easy to work out how much space the individual motifs will fill on the type of linen recommended.

	Pattern size 110 × 110 squares	Foxglove (see page 37) 169 × 65 squares
Linen 12 15 squares = 1 in	7 in × 7 in (18 × 18 cm)	11 × 4 in (28 × 10.5 cm)
Linen 10 13 1/8 squares = 1 in	8½ × 8½ in (21 × 21 cm)	13 × 5 in (32× 12 cm)
Linen 7 8 3/4 squares = 1 in	12½ × 12½ in (31.5 × 31.5 cm)	19 × 7½ in (48 × 18.5 cm)

This photograph shows the difference in size of a motif when worked on linen 12 and linen 7 respectively. The flower is Foxglove (Digitalis purpurea), which is reproduced in color on page 37. When worked on the coarse linen, the embroidery might well be used as a wall decoration.When worked on the normal, fine linen, it may be used for a place mat.

Method of working

The patterns in the book are done in cross-stitches. The different colors used are shown in symbols and numbers under the pattern diagrams. The photo on the opposite page shows the shades that are used and the colors of the Flower Thread with the appropriate numbers.

In certain patterns back-stitches are also used. The symbols are shown to the left of the cross-stitch symbols.

Cross-stich

A. Cross-stich from left to right. The under half of the stitch is made first, working crosswise over two threads of the linen from the lower left-hand corner to the upper right-hand corner. The upper half of the stitch is made backwards as shown.

B. Cross-stitch worked up and down. Each stitch is completed in one operation, so that the upper half of the stitch is in the same direction as in A. The wrong side of the work in both A and B appears as vertical rows of stitches.

C. Cross-stitches displaced in relation to each other.

D. Four ¾ cross-stitches are shown on the left. On the right can be seen half cross-stitches covering two threads length-wise and only one therad across.

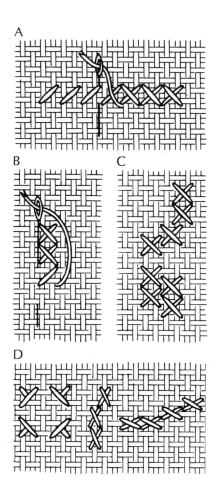

Back-stitch

A. Two different forms of back-stitch. In the left-hand illustration the upper stitches are made by inserting the needle two threads to the side and two threads down, one upright stitch passes over two threads and one horizontal stitch over two threads. In the right-hand illustration the upper stitch is made two threads down but only one to the side, and one of the stitches, the fourth, is made two threads to the side and one thread down.In addition one upright stitch and one horizontal stitch is shown.

B. Four back-stitchess sewn over a single thread and a single thread respctively intersection.

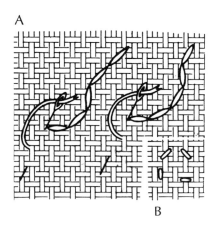

8

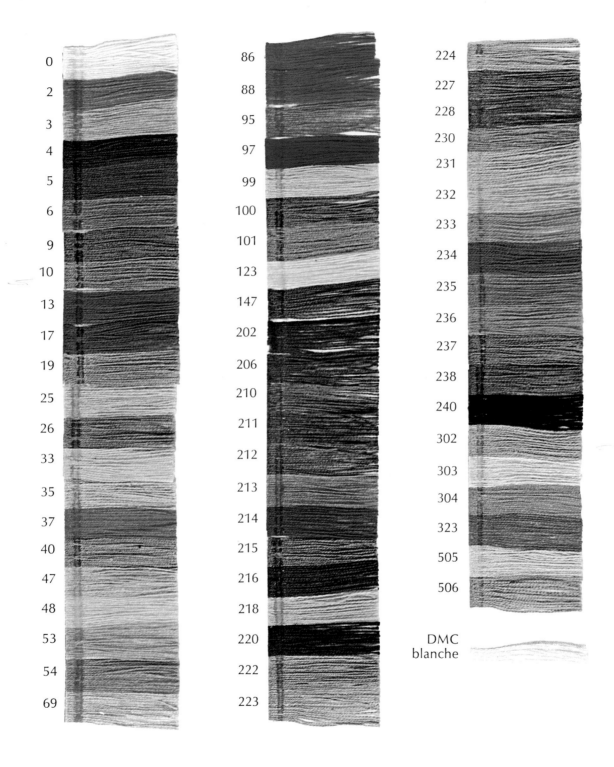

0	86	224
2	88	227
3	95	228
4	97	230
5	99	231
6	100	232
9	101	233
10	123	234
13	147	235
17	202	236
19	206	237
25	210	238
26	211	240
33	212	302
35	213	303
37	214	304
40	215	323
47	216	505
48	218	506
53	220	DMC blanche
54	222	
69	223	

The color key above to the Danish Handcraft Guild's Flower Thread indicates which colors have been used for the embroideries in the book.

9

Examples of finished work

The motifs in this book have a huge variety of uses, including place mats, doilies, runners, tea cosies, cushions, and wall hangings.

All the embroideries look best when mounted simply. The cushions are finished with matching piping. The runners and the various place mats are hem-stitched or bound discretely as shown on the place mat with Foxglove (see also page 37).

Runner with Woody Nightshade
Linen 12, bleached.
Cutting measurement: 13 × 40 in (32 × 100 cm).
Finished runner: 8½ × 36 in (21 × 90 cm).
Danish Flower Thread. Work with 1 strand.
Find center of motif by means of the arrows.
Find center line of linen by folding along its length.
Measure 5½ in (14 cm) in from the short edge. This point corresponds to the center of the motif. Begin here.
The distance between two motifs is 21 in (53 cm).
Hem-stitch over 3 threads. Hem: 7 threads wide.
Distance between embroidery and hem: 15 threads.

Cushion with Lesser Burdock
Linen 12, bleached.
Cutting measurement: 16 × 32 in (40 × 80 cm).
Finished cushion: 12 × 12 in (30 × 30 cm).
Danish Flower Thread. Work with 1 strand.
Divide the linen into two parts. Find center of motif by means of the arrows. Find center of linen and begin here.
Finish of the cushion with green piping.

Wall hanging – shown here with **Common Caraway, Blackthorn or Sloe, Broom and Dill** *respectively*.
Linen 12, bleached.
Cutting measurement: 13 × 13 in (32 × 32 cm).
Finished wall hanging: 9½ × 9½ in (24 × 24 cm).
Danish Flower Thread. Work with 1 strand.
Find center of motif by means of the arrows. Find center of linen and start here.

Place mat with Foxglove
Linen 12, bleached.
Cutting measurement: 16 × 21 in (40 × 53 cm).
Finished place mat: 12 × 16½ in (30 × 41 cm).
Danish Flower Thread. Work with 1 strand.
At upper left corner of linen, measure 2½ in (6 cm) along and down. Begin the border here.
Fold and turn under linen 7 threads from embroidery. Hem 7 threads wide.

Cushion with Borage
Linen 10, bleached.
Cutting measurement: 15 × 30 in (37 × 75 cm).
Finished cushion: 11½ × 11½ in (29 × 29 cm).
Danish Flower Thread. Work with 1 strand.
Divide the linen into two parts. Find center of motif by means of the arrows. Find center of linen and begin here.
Finish of the cushion with green piping.

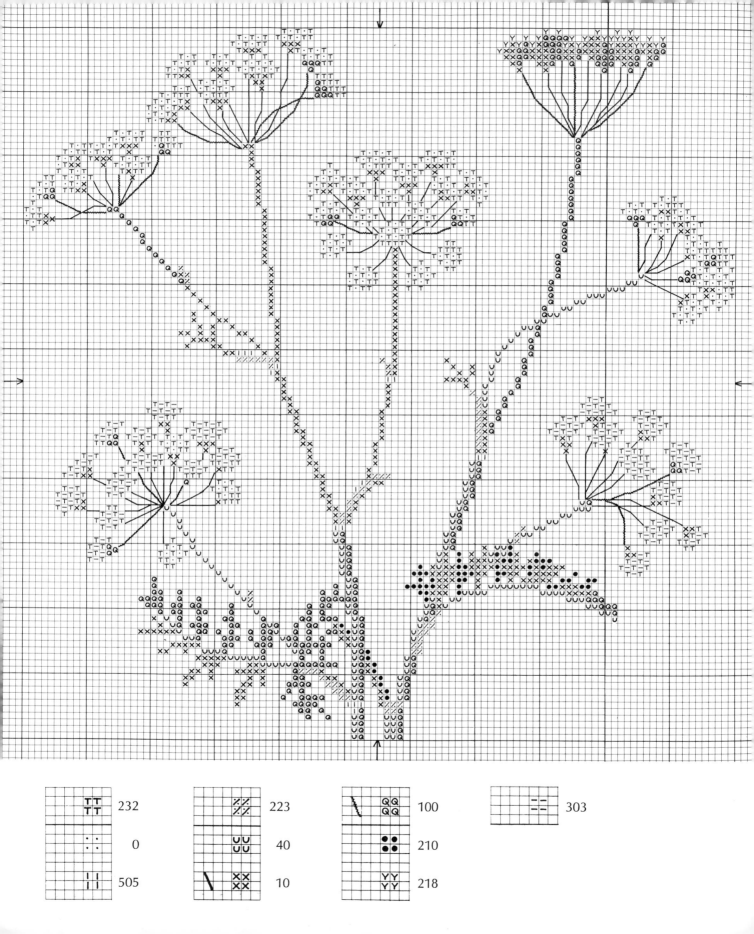

Burnet Saxifrage PIMPINELLA SAXIFRAGA
From the roots can be extracted drugs used as cough
drops and against hoarseness and coughing.

13

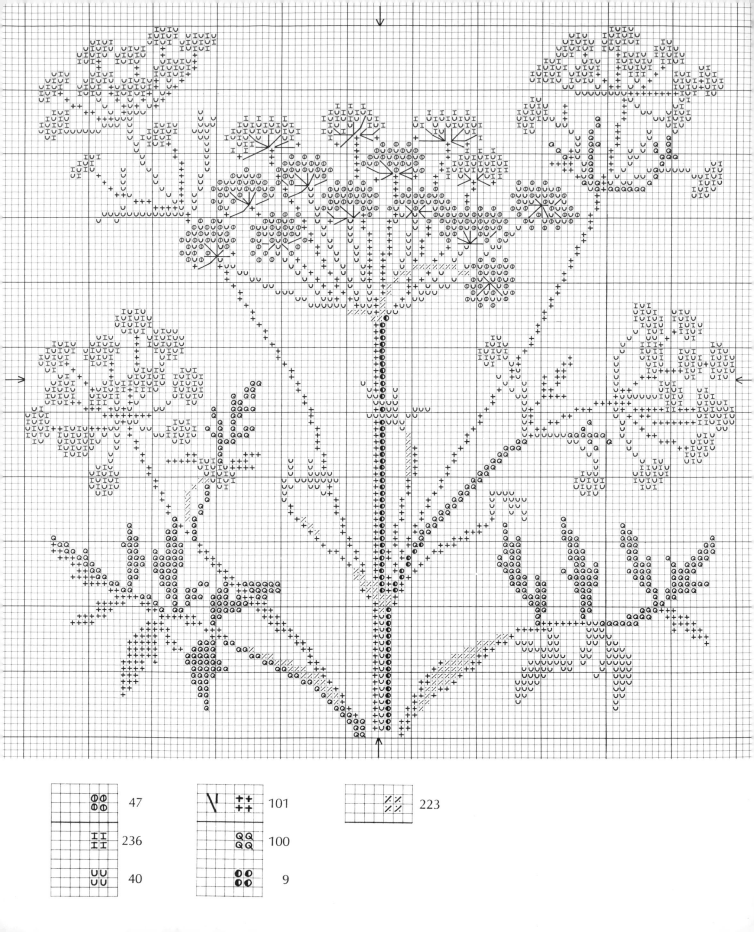

Wild Parsnip PASTINACA SATIVA
The juice of the roots can be used against toothache,
poisonous stings and bites.

15

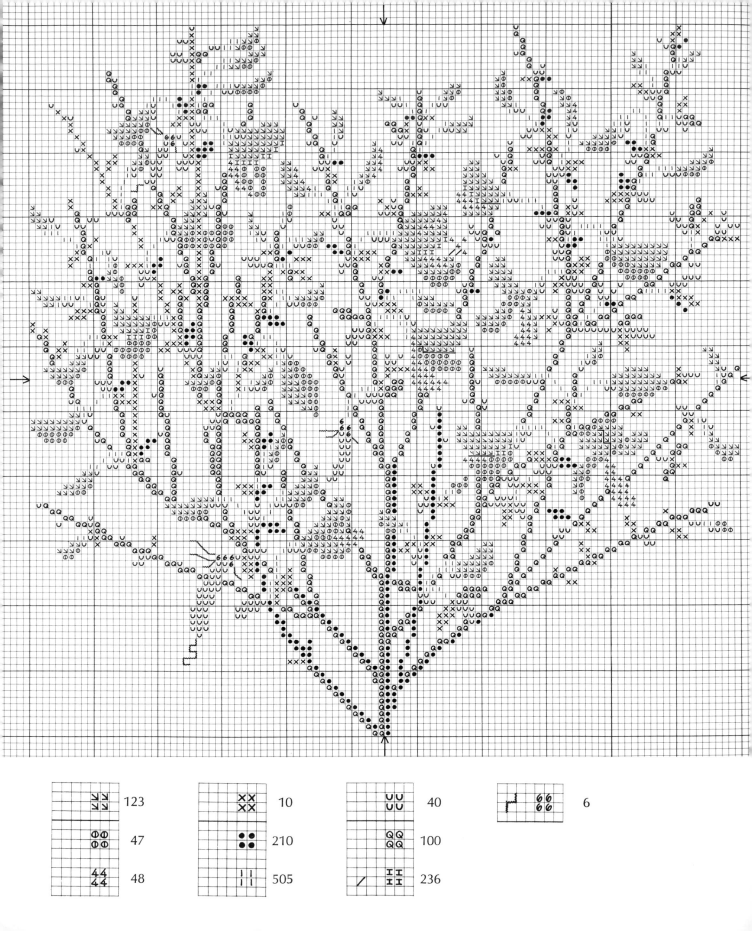

Broom SAROTHAMNUS SCOPARIUS †
From flowers and stalks can be extracted an uretic.   17

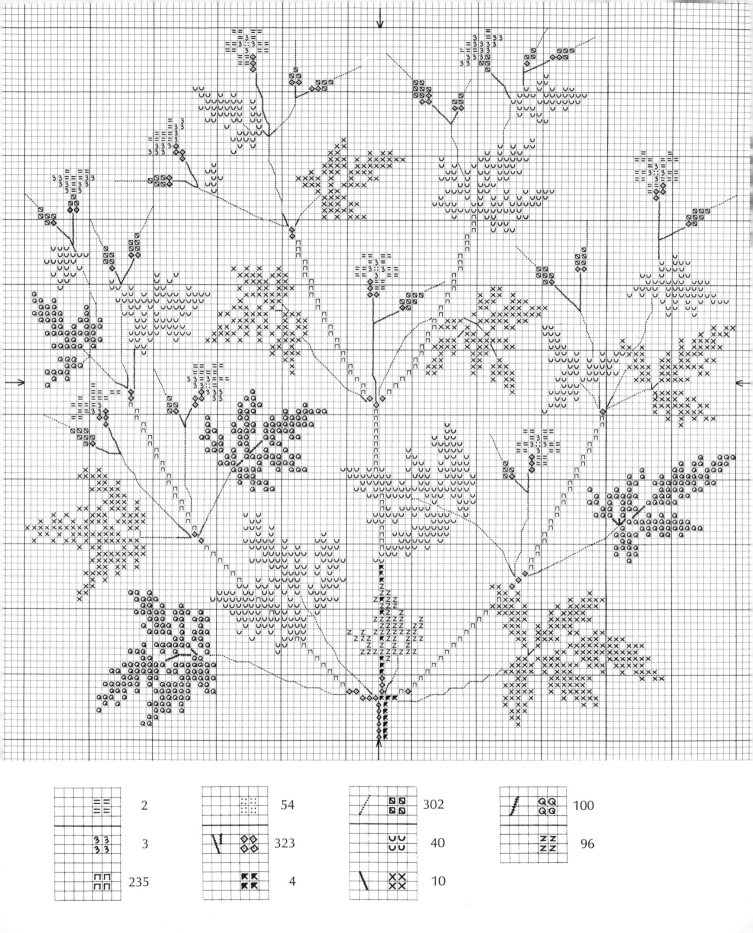

≡ ≡	2	
₃ ₃	3	
Π Π	235	

∷ ∷	54	
◇ ◇	323	
ⱪ ⱪ	4	

◨ ◨	302	
∪ ∪	40	
✕ ✕	10	

Q Q	100	
Z Z	96	

Herb Robert GERANIUM ROBERTIANUM
From stalks and leaves can be extracted a drug against
swelling of the uterus. Is used in perfume- and
soap manufacturing.

19

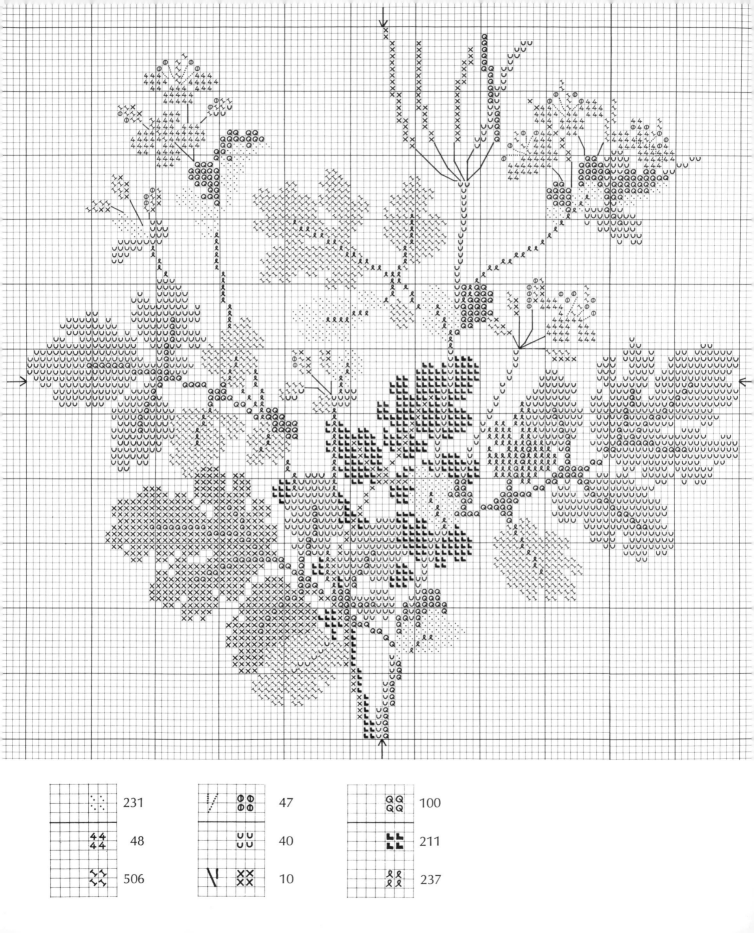

⠿ 231	⊕ 47	Q 100
4 48	∪ 40	L 211
⅄ 506	\ ✗ 10	ℓ 237

Greater Celandine CHELIDONIUM MAJUS
From the stalks can be extracted analgesics and
hypnotics as well as a remedy against jaundice.

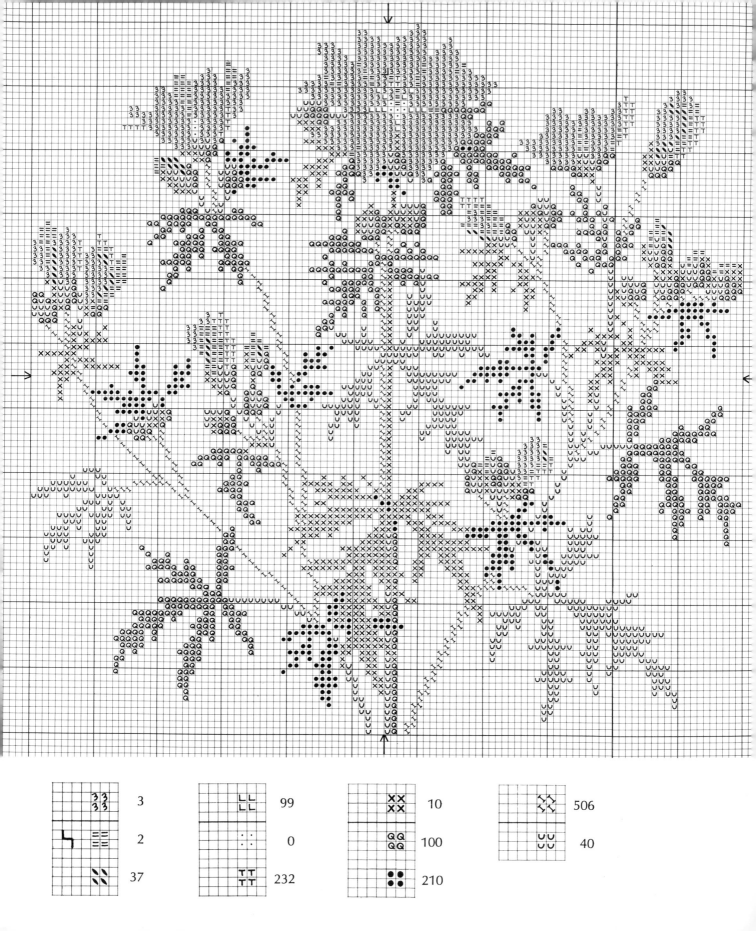

		3				L		99			X		10			↖ ↗		506
		2				·		0			Q		100			U		40
		37				T		232			●		210					

Musk Mallow MALVA MOSCHATA
From stalks and leaves can be extracted mucus
detaching drugs and laxatives. Can also be used
against nephritis and cystoliths as well as against
insomnia and headache.

23

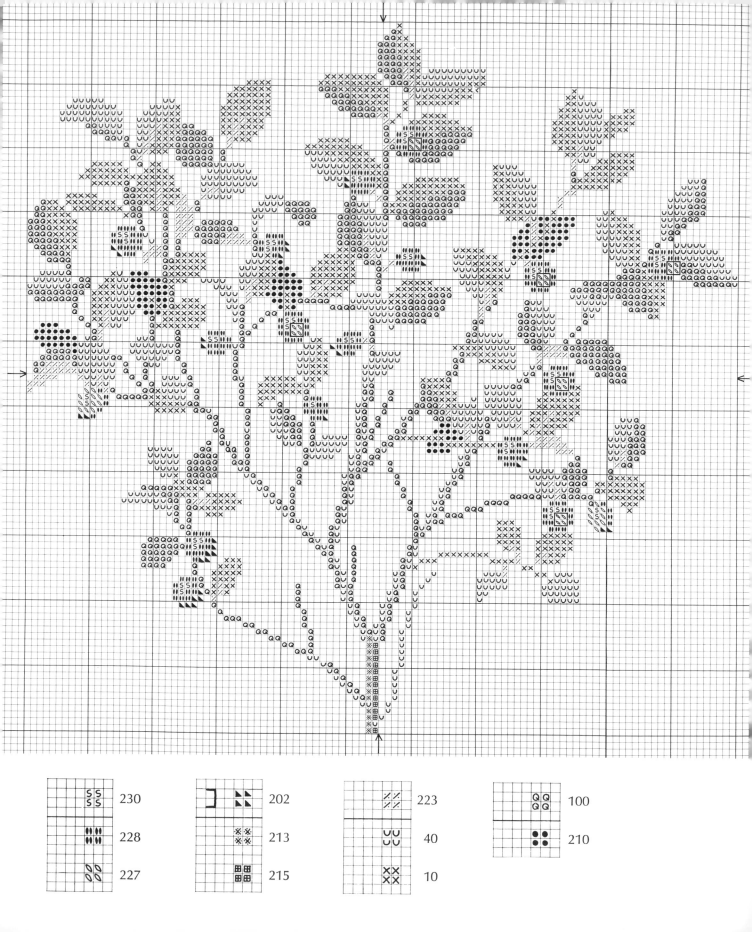

S S / S S	230	⌐ / ▲▲ / ▲▲	202	/ / / /	223
¦¦¦¦ / ¦¦¦¦	228	✕✕ / ✕✕	213	U U / U U	40
⦸⦸	227	⊞⊞ / ⊞⊞	215	✕✕ / ✕✕	10

Q Q / Q Q	100
●● / ●●	210

Bilberry or Whortleberry VACCINIUM MYRTILLUS
From the fruits can be extraced a drug against
diarrhoea and scurvy, and from the leaves a drug
against infections in the urinary system.

25

		505		XX	10		●●	210		⊓⊓	235		■■	240
				XX			●●			⊓⊓			■■	
	⅄⅄	506		LL	99		⌐⌐	5		++	101		♥♥	238
	⅄⅄			LL			⌐⌐			++			♥♥	
	UU	40		QQ	100		◇◇	323		◹◹	302		⟋⟋	35
	UU			QQ			◇◇			◹◹			⟋⟋	

Deadly Nightshade ATROPA BELLADONNA †
From stalks can be extracted a drug against nervous
asthma and neuralgia. Its fruits have abilities to
enlarge the pupils of the eyes.

	37		235		147		40		210
	4		19		223		10		232
	323		35		302		100		

Lesser Burdock ARCTIUM MINUS
The juice of the roots can be used against loss of hair,
podagra and rheumatism.

29

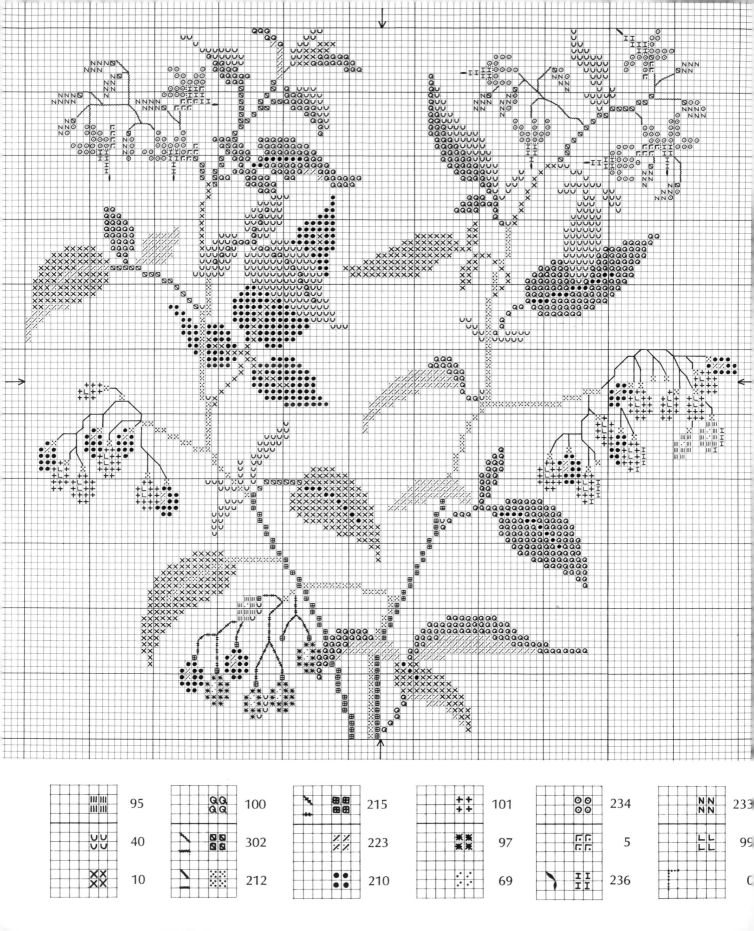

	95		100		215		101		234		233
	40		302		223		97		5		99
	10		212		210		69		236		

Woody Nightshade SOLANUM DULCAMARA †
From young stalks and roots can be extracted
blood-cleansing and sudorific drugs.

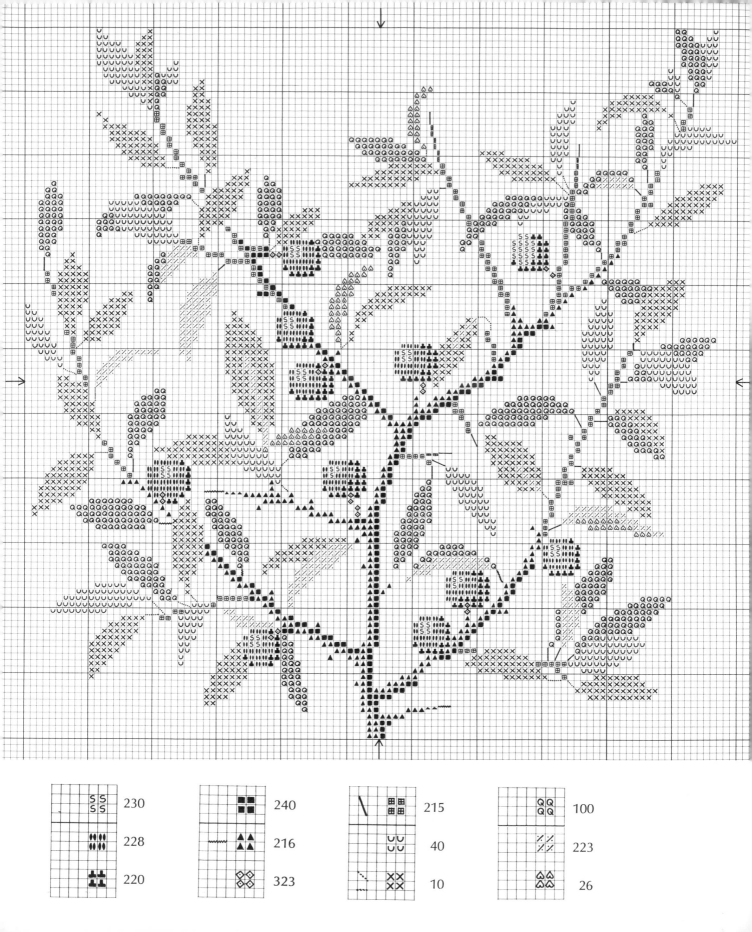

	S S		
	S S	230	

	● ●		
	● ●	240	

╲	⊞ ⊞		
	⊞ ⊞	215	

	Q Q		
	Q Q	100	

	▮▮		
	▮▮	228	

∿	▲ ▲		
	▲ ▲	216	

	U U		
	U U	40	

	⁄ ⁄		
	⁄ ⁄	223	

	♣♣		
	♣♣	220	

	◇ ◇		
	◇ ◇	323	

⋯	X X		
∿	X X	10	

	⌂ ⌂		
	⌂ ⌂	26	

Blackthorn or Sloe PRUNUS SPINOSA
From the fruits can be extracted a drug used as a mild
laxative.

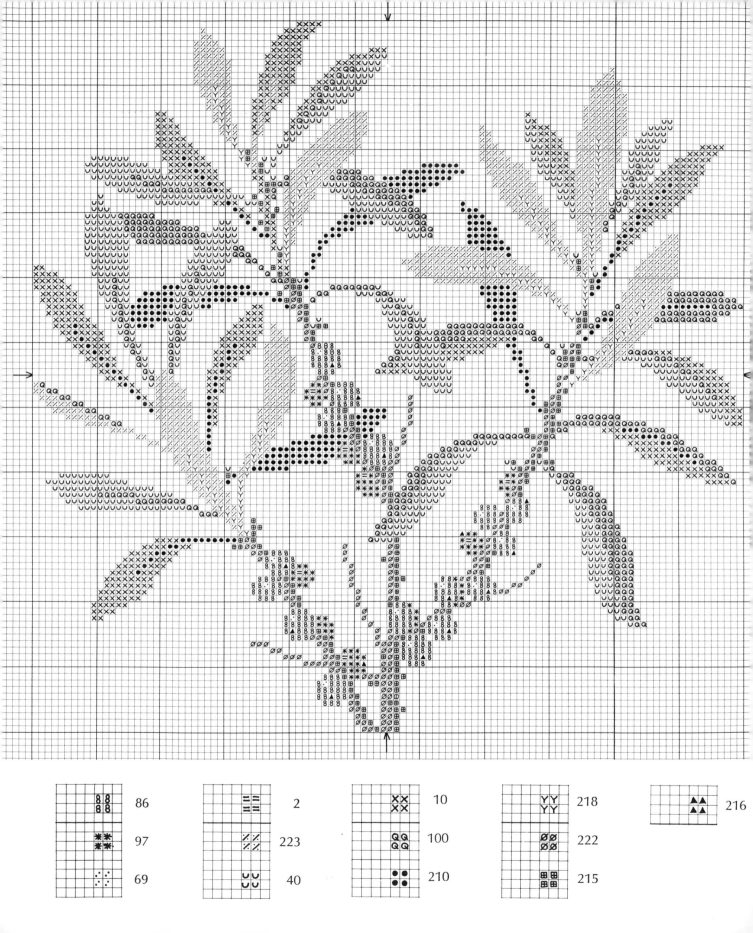

	86		2		10		218		216
	97		223		100		222		
	69		40		210		215		

Mezereon DAPHNE MEZEREUM †
From berries and bark can be extracted an emetic.   35

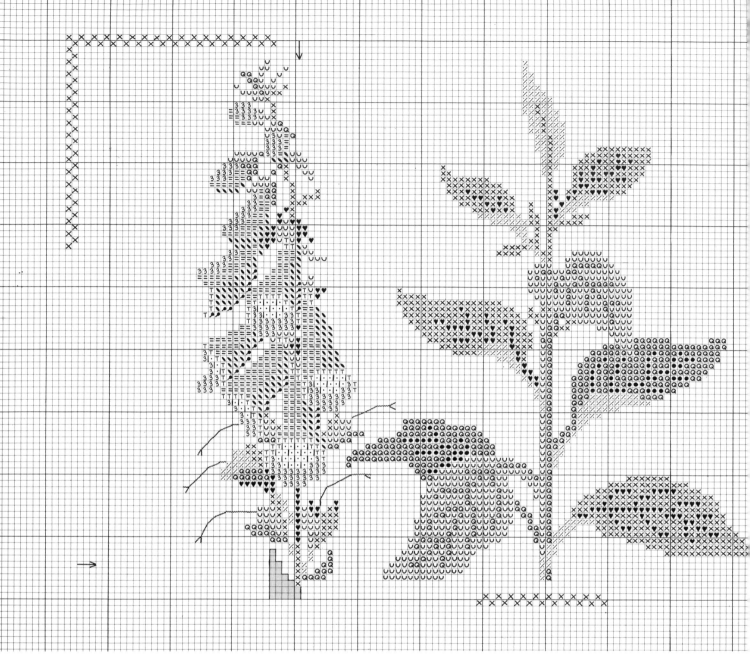

*The Foxglove (Digitalis purpurea) can be worked as a
tall plant (see, for example, page 7). The shaded area on
the bottom left of the pattern indicates how to continue
with the right-hand side of the pattern.*

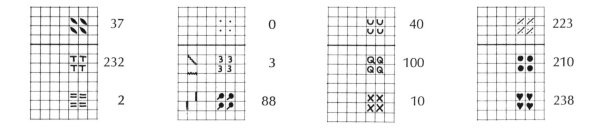

◥◥	37	
◥◥		
T T	232	
T T		
= =	2	
= =		

· ·	0	
· ·		
3 3	3	
3 3		
◢◢	88	
◢◢		

U U	40	
U U		
Q Q	100	
Q Q		
X X	10	
X X		

⁄⁄	223	
⁄⁄		
● ●	210	
● ●		
♥ ♥	238	
♥ ♥		

Foxglove DIGITALIS PURPUREA †
From the leaves can be extracted a drug against heart
diseases, and it can also heal wounds.

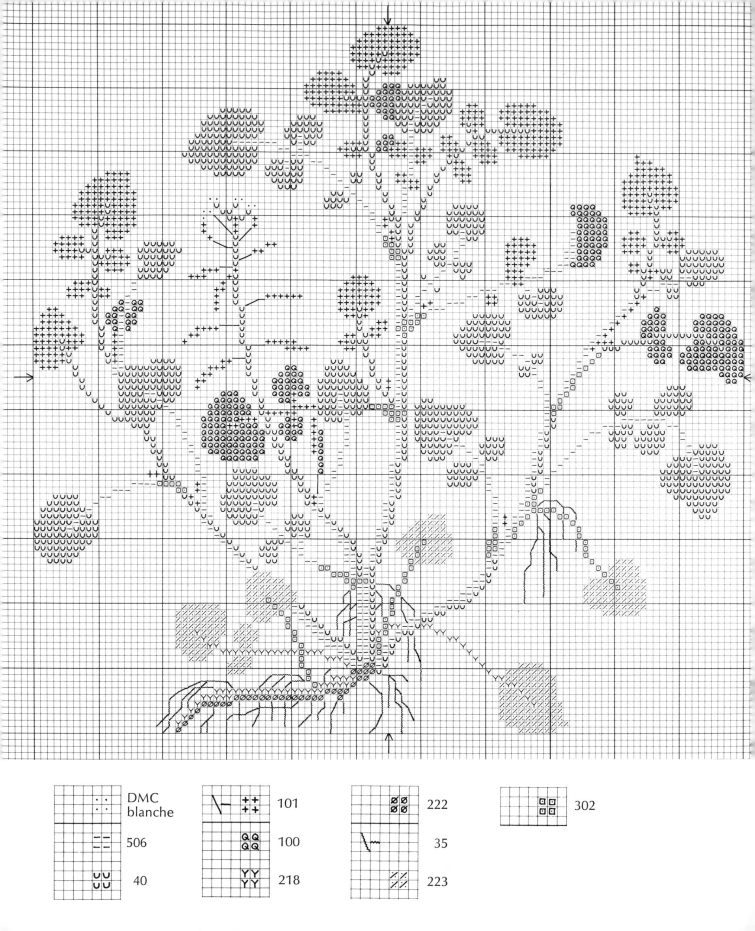

· · / ·	DMC blanche		
− −	506		
U U	40		

＼ − / + + / + +	101		
Q Q / Q Q	100		
Y Y / Y Y	218		

Ø Ø / Ø Ø	222		
\ m	35		
∕ ∕ / ∕ ∕	223		

□ □ / □ □	302

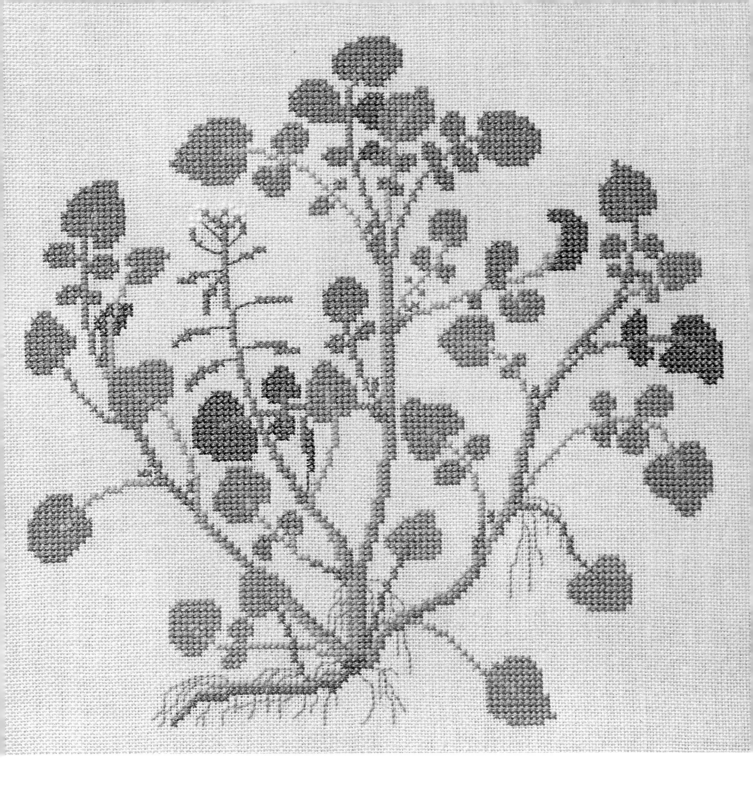

Watercress NASTURTIUM OFFICINALIS
Difficult to cultivate. Grows wild in a few places in
Denmark. Can be eaten fresh with meat dishes.

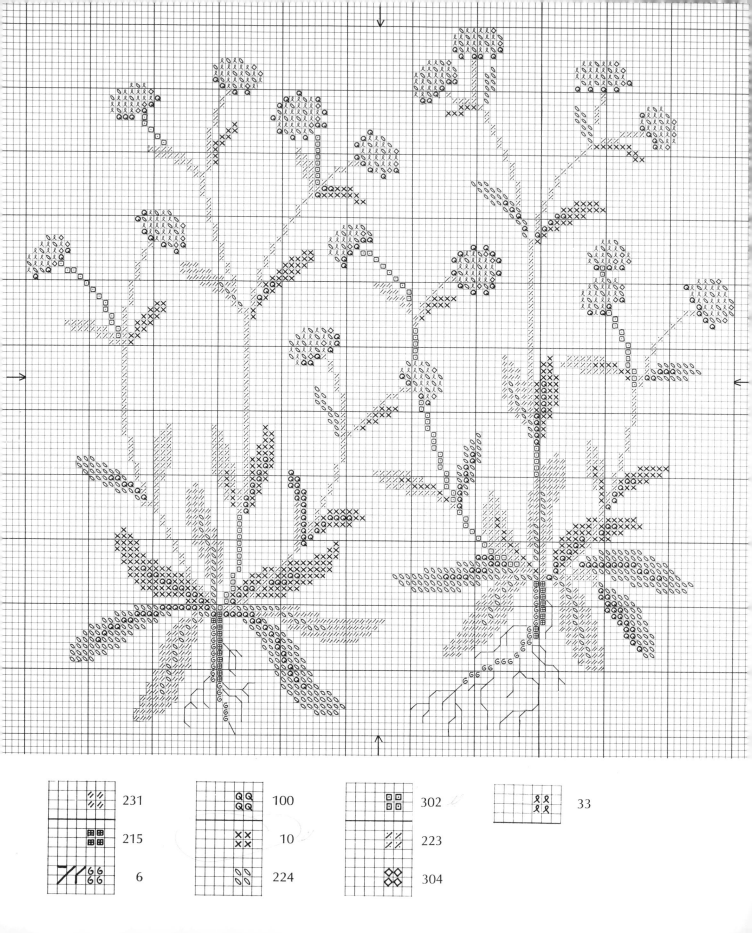

	231
	215
	6

	100
	10
	224

	302
	223
	304

| | 33 |

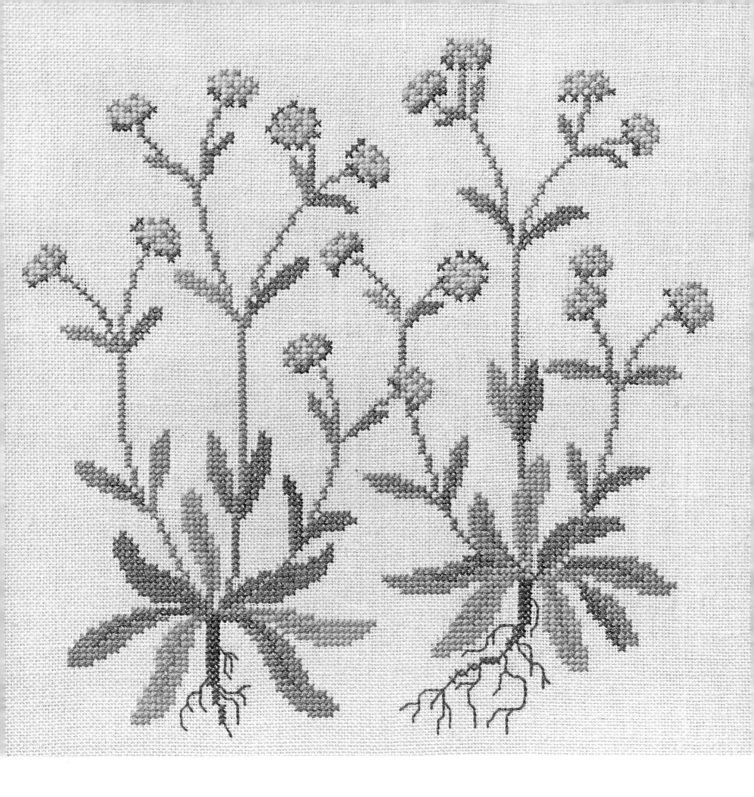

Lamb's Lettuce VALERIANELLA LOCUSTA
Grows wild in many places. Has thick, juicy leaves
and a crisp stem, which can be eaten fresh in salads.

41

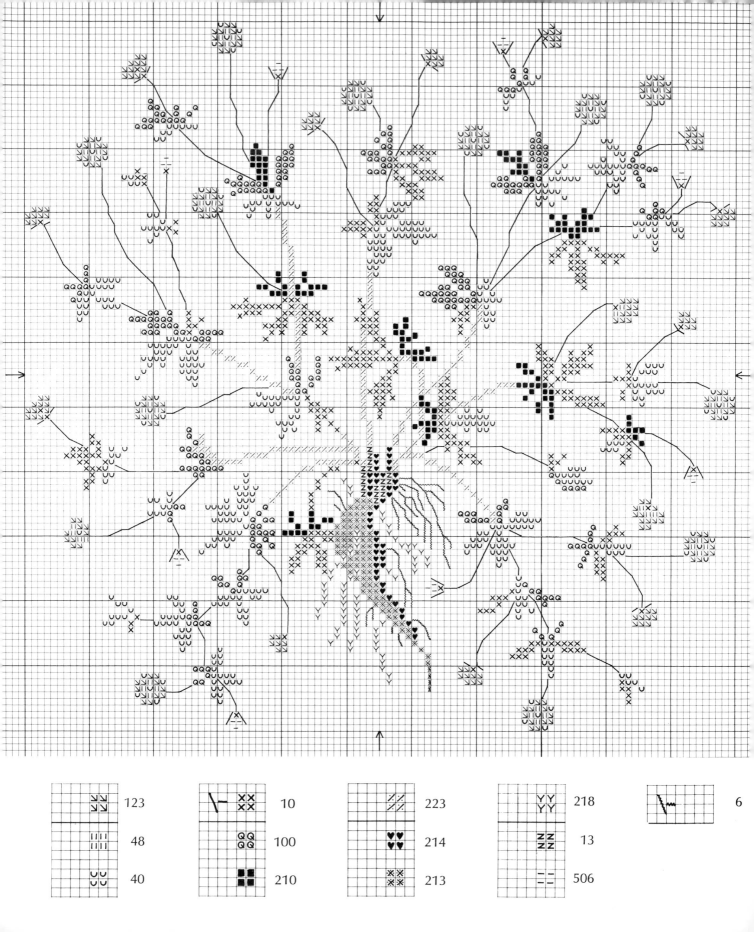

	123		10		223		218		6
	48		100		214		13		
	40		210		213		506		

Common Tormentil POTENTILLA ERECTA
Grows in sandy areas. The root can be put in snaps.   43

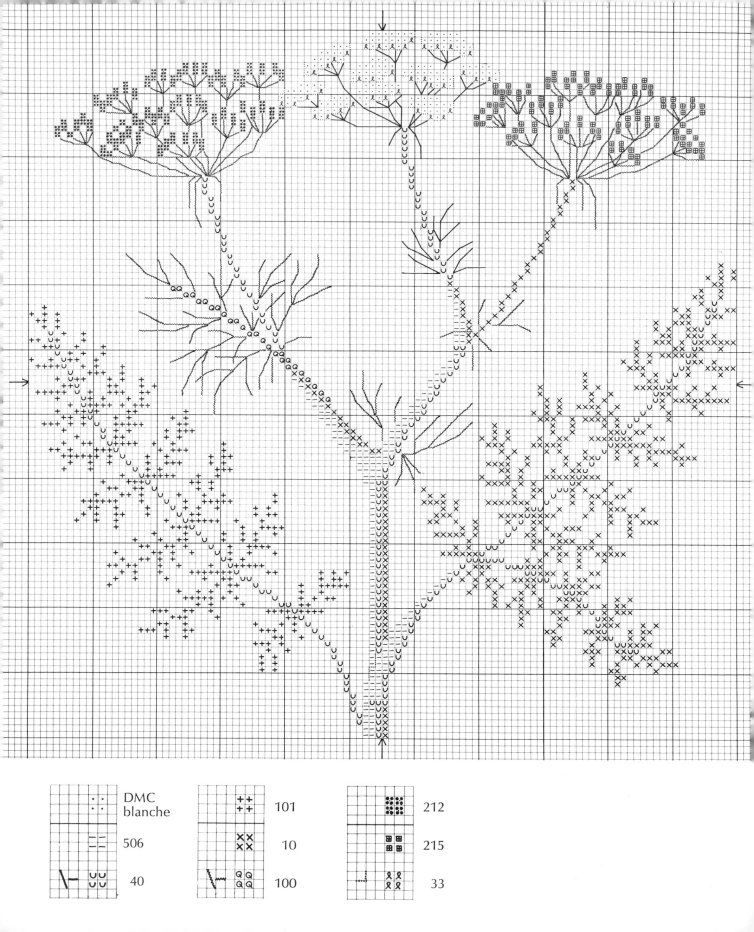

	DMC blanche			101			212
	506			10			215
	40			100			33

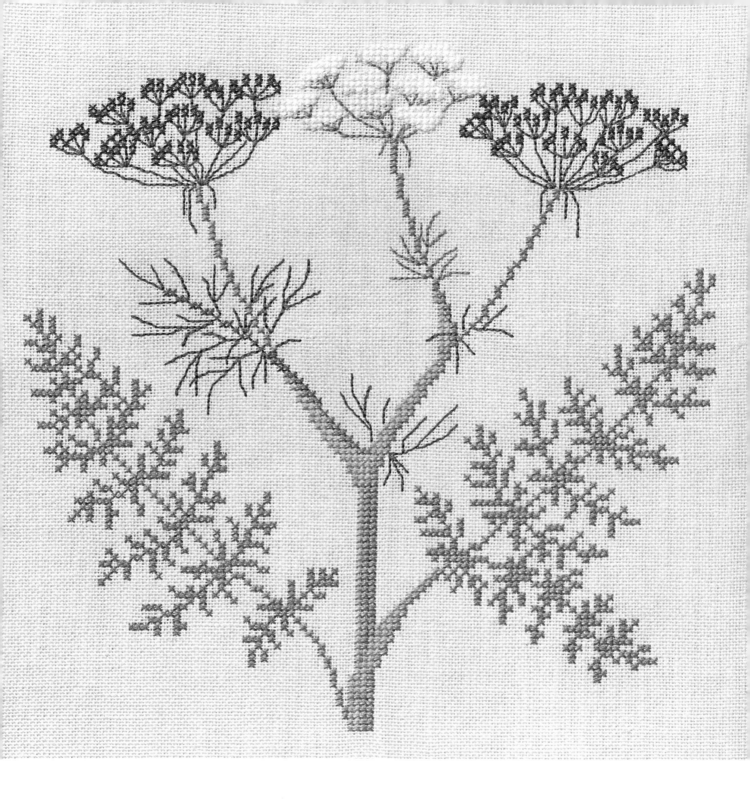

Common Caraway CARUM CARVI
Hardy plant, which is easy to grow. Seeds itself. Is one
of the most common herbs.

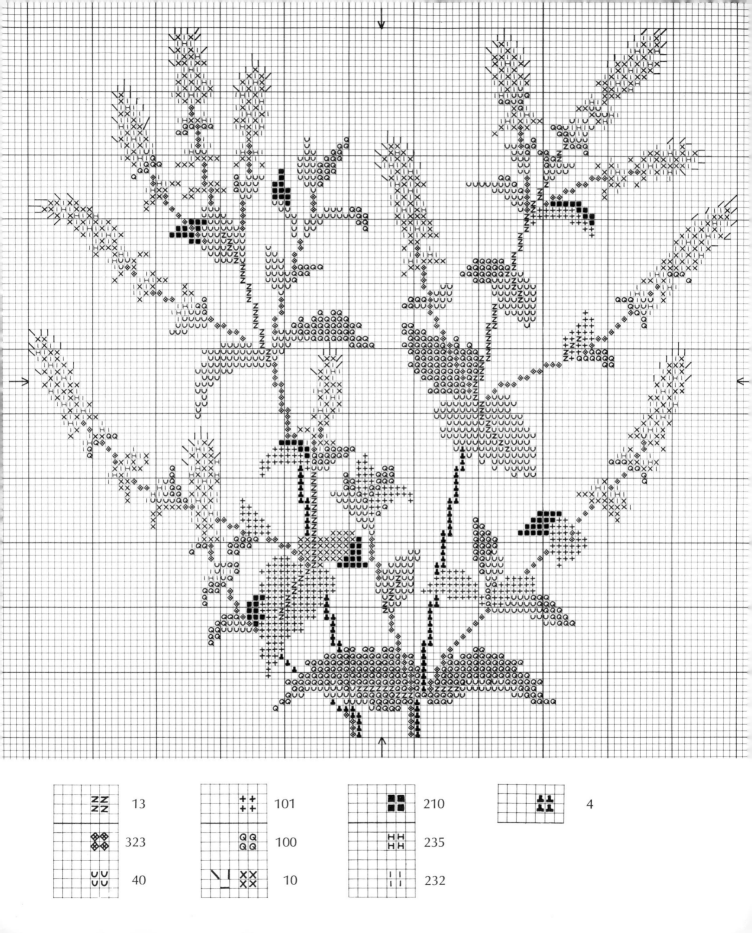

Pepper Mint MENTHA PIPERITA, VAR. CRISPULA
Easy to grow. Has a tendency to spread. May also be
used for lamb dishes.

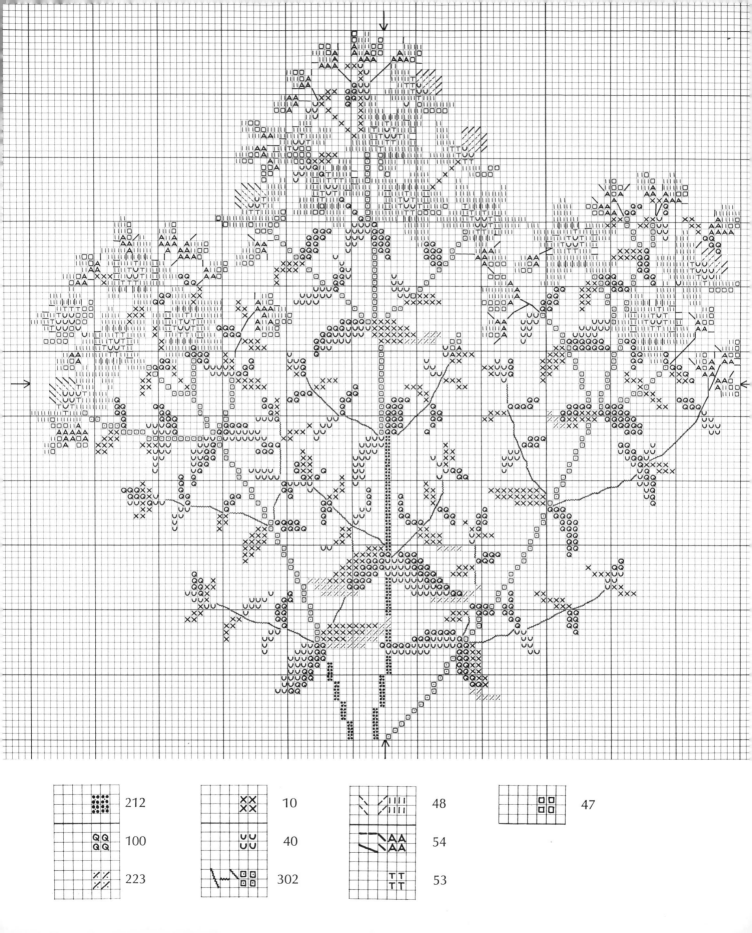

	212		10		48		47
	100		40		54		
	223		302		53		

Perforate St.-John's-Wort HYPERICUM PERFORATUM
Grows throughout Denmark. Leave the flowers and
buds to draw for a couple of months in snaps in order
to obtain red, tasty pericum snaps.

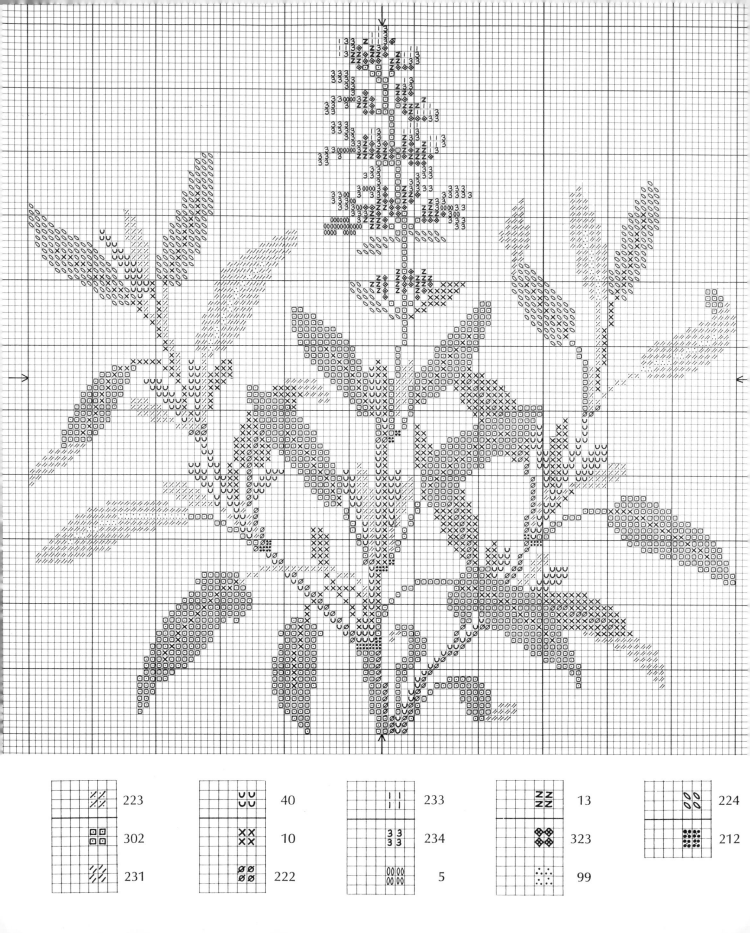

223	40	233	13	224
302	10	234	323	212
231	222	5	99	

Sage SALVIA OFFICINALIS
Also called "donkey's ear" because of its gray, hairy leaves. Comes from the Mediterranean. Strong tasting, should be used sparingly. Counteracts some of the fishy smell of sea-birds.

51

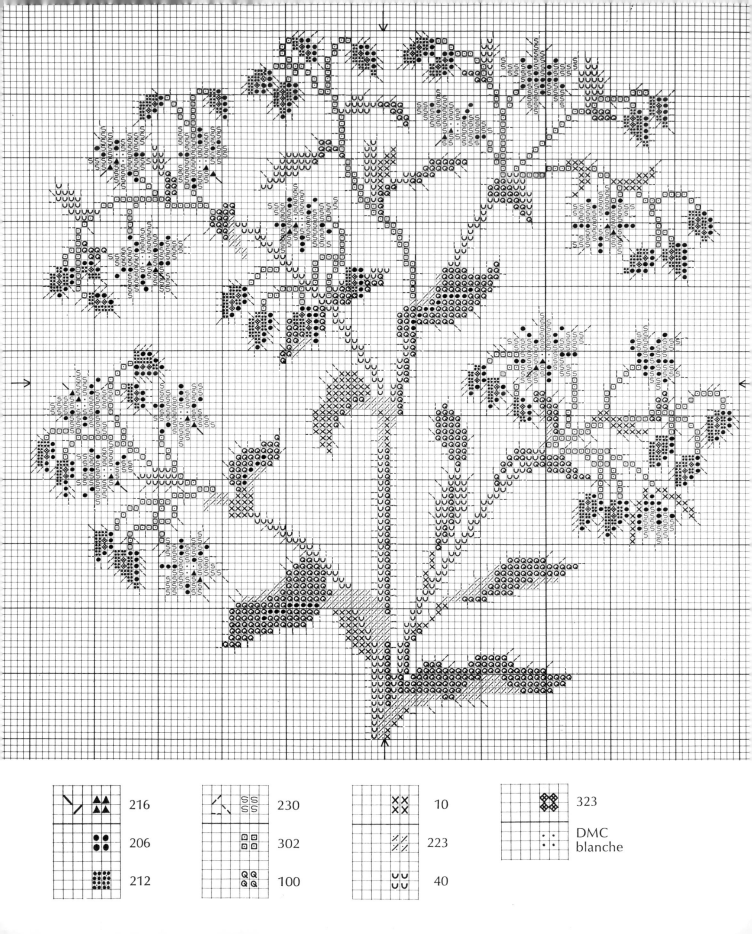

	216		230		10		323
	206		302		223		DMC blanche
	212		100		40		

Borage BORAGO OFFICINALIS
Hardy plant. Can be harvested until the frost starts.
Leaves and flowers may be used in salads.

53

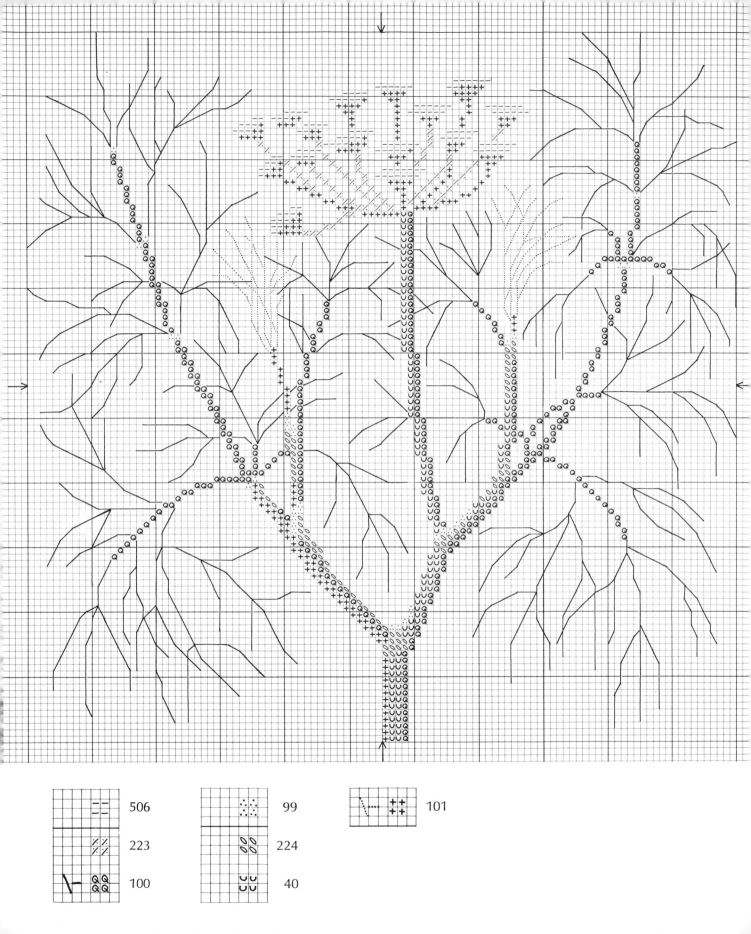

– –	506	∵∵	99	＼•• ++ 101
⁒⁒	223	∅∅	224	
＼ QQ QQ	100	∪∪	40	

Dill ANETHUM GRAVEOLENS
One of the most common Danish culinary herbs. Easy
to grow. Used especially for fish dishes. The seeds
contain oil, which is used in the perfume and soap
industry.

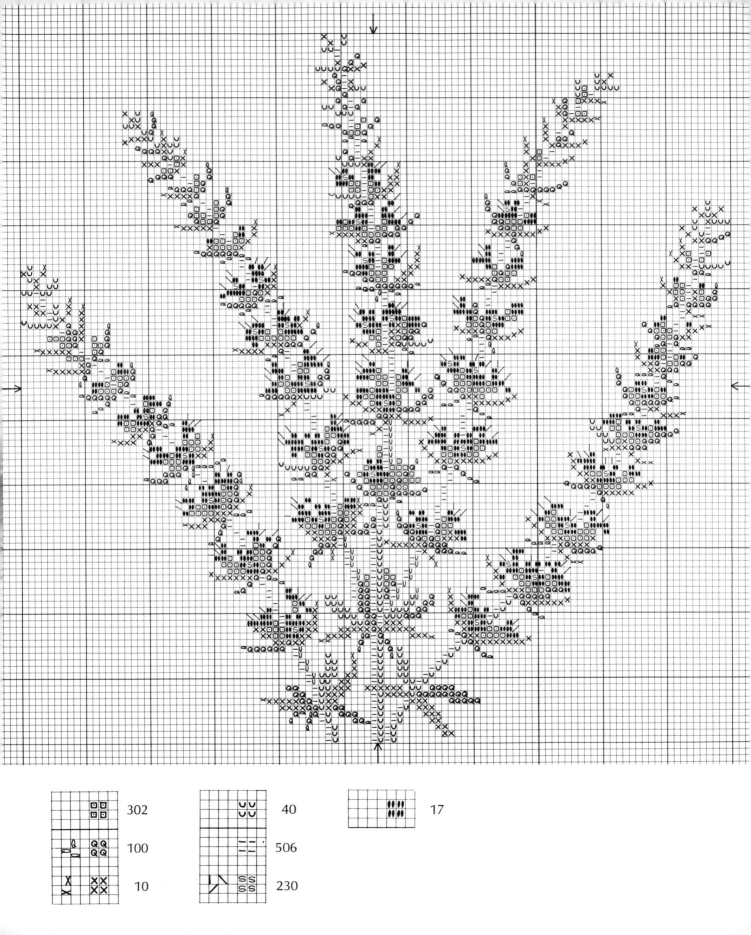

	302
	100
	10

	40
	506
	230

| | 17 |

Hyssop HYSSOPUS OFFICINALIS
Common Danish perennial. Useful in a bouquet
garni, although a little bitter.

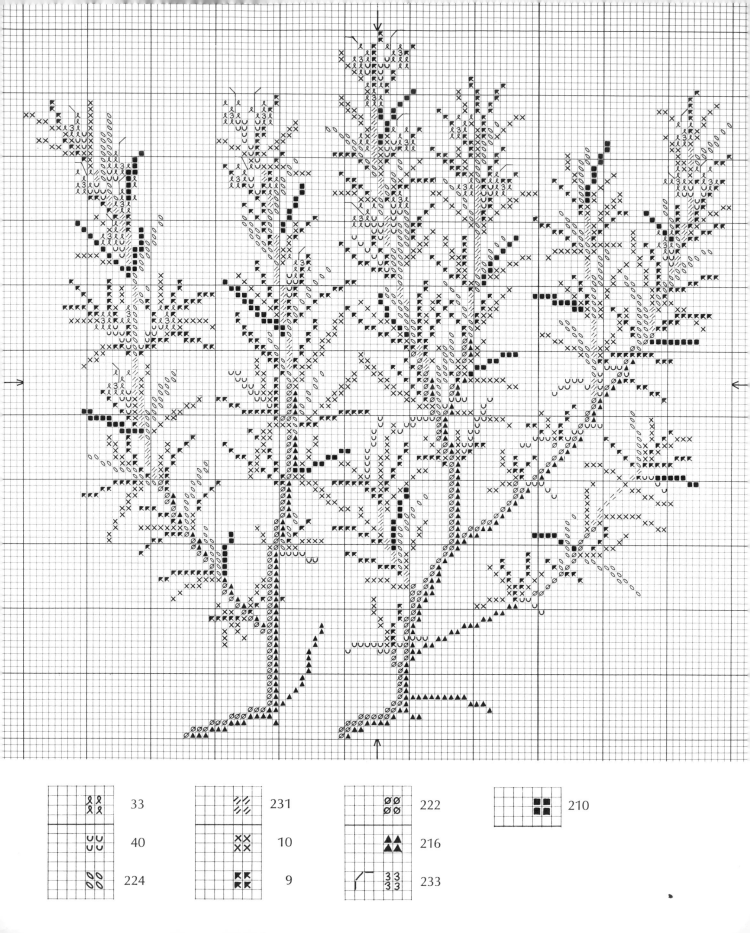

	33		231		222		210
	40		10		216		
	224		9		233		

Rosemary ROSMARINUS OFFICINALIS
Grows wild in the Mediterranean scrub. The leaves
contain oil, which is used in the perfume and soap
industry. Suitable for roast pork and rich fish dishes.

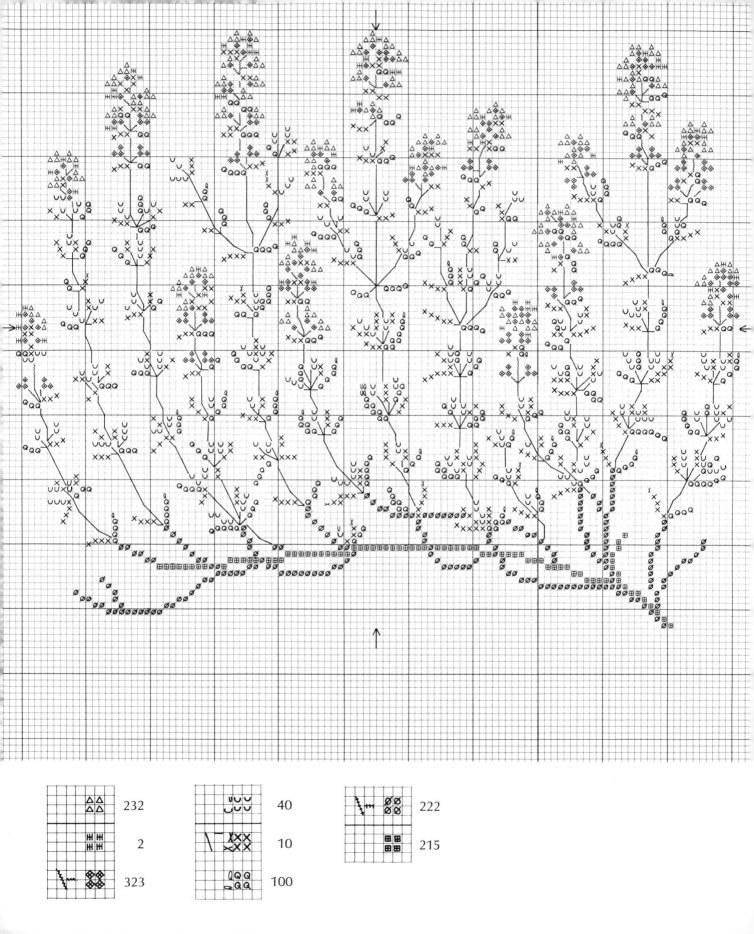

		232
		2
		323

		40
		10
		100

| | | 222 |
| | | 215 |

Thyme THYMUS VULGARIS
Grows wild in the Mediterranean scrub but is
commonly grown in Denmark. Very suitable for
vegetable soups and lamb.

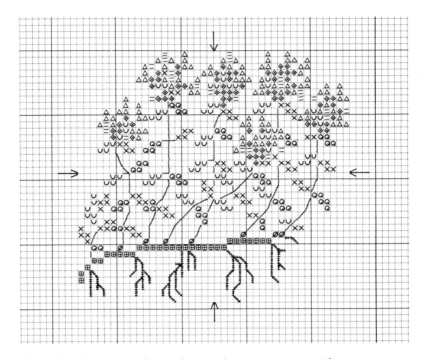

*The little thyme motif may be used as a corner motif
for a place mat.*

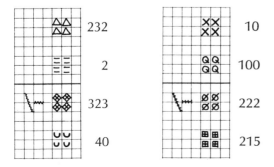

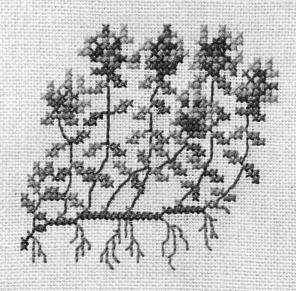

Wild Thyme THYMUS SERPYLLUM
Wild thyme grows on windswept hills, heaths and
dunes. It was once popular as a medicine and herb.

List of patterns

Medicinal plants

Bilberry or Whortleberry *(Vaccinium myrtillus)*   25
Blackthorn or Sloe *(Prunus spinosa)*   33
Broom *(Sarothamnus scoparius)*†   17
Burnet Saxifrage *(Pimpinella saxifraga)*   13
Deadly Nightshade *(Atropa belladonna)*†   27
Foxglove *(Digitalis purpurea)*† 37
Greater Celandine *(Chelidonium majus)*   21
Herb Robert *(Geranium robertianum)*   19
Lesser Burdock *(Arctium minus)*   29
Mezereon *(Daphne mezereum)*† 35
Musk Mallow *(Malva moschata)*   23
Wild Parsnip *(Pastinaca sativa)*   15
Woody Nightshade *(Solanum dulcamara)*† 31

Culinary Herbs

Borage *(Borago officinalis)*   53
Common Caraway *(Carum carvi)*   45
Common Tormentil *(Potentilla erecta)*   43
Dill *(Anethum graveolens)*   55
Hyssop *(Hyssopus officinalis)*   57
Lamb's Lettuce *(Valerianella locusta)*   41
Pepper Mint *(Mentha piperita, var. crispula)*   47
Perforate St.-John's-Worth *(Hypericum perforatum)*   49
Rosemary *(Rosmarinus officinalis)*   59
Sage *(Salvia officinalis)*   51
Thyme *(Thymus vulgaris)*   61
Watercress *(Nasturtium officinalis)*   39
Wild Thyme *(Thymus serpyllum)*   63

† = poisonous plants

Suppliers

These suppliers sell wholesale only. They will be happy to supply you with a list of retail outlets in your area that carry cross-stitch materials.

Counted Thread Society of America
3305 South Newport Street
Denver, CO 80222

Cross Stitch Country, Inc.
P.O.B. 825
Pawleys Island, SC 29585
(Supplier of Danish Flower Thread)

Joan Toggit
246 Fifth Avenue
New York, NY 10001

PRINTED IN D
PERMILD & R